Vehicle Maintenance Log

Vehicle _____

Maintenance Years

_____ to_____

Ideas for using this book:

Cover and first page: Fill in Vehicle (make and model or nickname). Fill in Maintenance Years (2015 to 2019 etc.). The years are there in case you need a second volume down the road.

Vehicle Notes: Record anything you want to remember about the car, purchase details, modifications, accidents etc.

Fuel Stops, Oil Changes, Transmission Fluid, Differential Fluid, Tire Maintenance, Tires and Other Maintenance: Fill out information as performed. For Other Maintenance log windshield wipers, headlights, fuses etc.

Graphs: Grids to chart mileage per gallon, price of gas per a gallon or anything else.

Contacts: A place to record people you meet who did or might do work on your vehicle in the future, or anyone you meet related to your vehicle.

Vehicle Maintenance Log should hold a few years of maintenance for the average vehicle. Looking for something smaller, check out the *1 Year Vehicle Maintenance Log*.

Copyright © S M

Table of Contents

Vehicle Notes

Vehicle Notes

_____

_____

_____

_____

_____

_____

_____

_____

_____

_____

_____

_____

_____

_____

_____

_____

Vehicle Notes

_____

_____

_____

_____

_____

_____

_____

_____

_____

_____

_____

_____

_____

_____

_____

_____

_____

_____

Vehicle Notes

_____

_____

_____

_____

_____

_____

_____

_____

_____

_____

_____

_____

_____

_____

_____

_____

Fuel
Stops

Date _____ Mileage_____
Fuel Amount Added _____
Price per Gallon _____
Miles per Gallon _____
Gas Station or Brand _____

_____

Date _____ Mileage_____
Fuel Amount Added _____
Price per Gallon _____
Miles per Gallon _____
Gas Station or Brand _____

_____

Date _____ Mileage_____
Fuel Amount Added _____
Price per Gallon _____
Miles per Gallon _____
Gas Station or Brand _____

_____

Date _____ Mileage_____
Fuel Amount Added _____
Price per Gallon _____
Miles per Gallon _____
Gas Station or Brand _____

_____

Date _____ Mileage_____
Fuel Amount Added _____
Price per Gallon _____
Miles per Gallon _____
Gas Station or Brand _____

_____

Date _____ Mileage_____
Fuel Amount Added _____
Price per Gallon _____
Miles per Gallon _____
Gas Station or Brand _____

_____

Date _____ Mileage_____
Fuel Amount Added _____
Price per Gallon _____
Miles per Gallon _____
Gas Station or Brand _____

_____

Date _____ Mileage_____
Fuel Amount Added _____
Price per Gallon _____
Miles per Gallon _____
Gas Station or Brand _____

_____

Fuel Stops

Date _____ Mileage_____
Fuel Amount Added _____
Price per Gallon _____
Miles per Gallon _____
Gas Station or Brand _____

_____

Date _____ Mileage_____
Fuel Amount Added _____
Price per Gallon _____
Miles per Gallon _____
Gas Station or Brand _____

_____

Date _____ Mileage_____
Fuel Amount Added _____
Price per Gallon _____
Miles per Gallon _____
Gas Station or Brand _____

_____

Fuel Stops

Date _____ Mileage_____
Fuel Amount Added _____
Price per Gallon _____
Miles per Gallon _____
Gas Station or Brand _____

_____

Date _____ Mileage_____
Fuel Amount Added _____
Price per Gallon _____
Miles per Gallon _____
Gas Station or Brand _____

_____

Date _____ Mileage_____
Fuel Amount Added _____
Price per Gallon _____
Miles per Gallon _____
Gas Station or Brand _____

_____

Fuel Stops

Date _____ Mileage_____
Fuel Amount Added _____
Price per Gallon _____
Miles per Gallon _____
Gas Station or Brand _____

_____

Date _____ Mileage_____
Fuel Amount Added _____
Price per Gallon _____
Miles per Gallon _____
Gas Station or Brand _____

_____

Date _____ Mileage_____
Fuel Amount Added _____
Price per Gallon _____
Miles per Gallon _____
Gas Station or Brand _____

_____

Date _____ Mileage_____
Fuel Amount Added _____
Price per Gallon _____
Miles per Gallon _____
Gas Station or Brand _____

_____

Date _____ Mileage_____
Fuel Amount Added _____
Price per Gallon _____
Miles per Gallon _____
Gas Station or Brand _____

_____

Date _____ Mileage_____
Fuel Amount Added _____
Price per Gallon _____
Miles per Gallon _____
Gas Station or Brand _____

_____

Fuel Stops

Date _____ Mileage_____
Fuel Amount Added _____
Price per Gallon _____
Miles per Gallon _____
Gas Station or Brand _____

_____

Date _____ Mileage_____
Fuel Amount Added _____
Price per Gallon _____
Miles per Gallon _____
Gas Station or Brand _____

_____

Date _____ Mileage_____
Fuel Amount Added _____
Price per Gallon _____
Miles per Gallon _____
Gas Station or Brand _____

_____

Date _____ Mileage_____

Fuel Amount Added _____

Price per Gallon _____

Miles per Gallon _____

Gas Station or Brand _____

_____

Date _____ Mileage_____

Fuel Amount Added _____

Price per Gallon _____

Miles per Gallon _____

Gas Station or Brand _____

_____

Date _____ Mileage_____

Fuel Amount Added _____

Price per Gallon _____

Miles per Gallon _____

Gas Station or Brand _____

_____

Date _____ Mileage_____

Fuel Amount Added _____

Price per Gallon _____

Miles per Gallon _____

Gas Station or Brand _____

_____

Date _____ Mileage_____

Fuel Amount Added _____

Price per Gallon _____

Miles per Gallon _____

Gas Station or Brand _____

_____

Date _____ Mileage_____

Fuel Amount Added _____

Price per Gallon _____

Miles per Gallon _____

Gas Station or Brand _____

_____

Date _____ Mileage_____
Fuel Amount Added _____
Price per Gallon _____
Miles per Gallon _____
Gas Station or Brand _____

_____

Date _____ Mileage_____
Fuel Amount Added _____
Price per Gallon _____
Miles per Gallon _____
Gas Station or Brand _____

_____

Date _____ Mileage_____
Fuel Amount Added _____
Price per Gallon _____
Miles per Gallon _____
Gas Station or Brand _____

_____

Fuel Stops

Date _____ Mileage_____
Fuel Amount Added _____
Price per Gallon _____
Miles per Gallon _____
Gas Station or Brand _____

_____

Date _____ Mileage_____
Fuel Amount Added _____
Price per Gallon _____
Miles per Gallon _____
Gas Station or Brand _____

_____

Date _____ Mileage_____
Fuel Amount Added _____
Price per Gallon _____
Miles per Gallon _____
Gas Station or Brand _____

_____

Fuel Stops

Date _____ Mileage_____

Fuel Amount Added _____

Price per Gallon _____

Miles per Gallon _____

Gas Station or Brand _____

_____

Date _____ Mileage_____

Fuel Amount Added _____

Price per Gallon _____

Miles per Gallon _____

Gas Station or Brand _____

_____

Date _____ Mileage_____

Fuel Amount Added _____

Price per Gallon _____

Miles per Gallon _____

Gas Station or Brand _____

_____

Fuel Stops

Date _____ Mileage_____

Fuel Amount Added _____

Price per Gallon _____

Miles per Gallon _____

Gas Station or Brand _____

_____

Date _____ Mileage_____

Fuel Amount Added _____

Price per Gallon _____

Miles per Gallon _____

Gas Station or Brand _____

_____

Date _____ Mileage_____

Fuel Amount Added _____

Price per Gallon _____

Miles per Gallon _____

Gas Station or Brand _____

_____

Date _____ Mileage_____
Fuel Amount Added _____
Price per Gallon _____
Miles per Gallon _____
Gas Station or Brand _____

_____

Date _____ Mileage_____
Fuel Amount Added _____
Price per Gallon _____
Miles per Gallon _____
Gas Station or Brand _____

_____

Date _____ Mileage_____
Fuel Amount Added _____
Price per Gallon _____
Miles per Gallon _____
Gas Station or Brand _____

_____

Fuel Stops

Date _____ Mileage_____

Fuel Amount Added _____

Price per Gallon _____

Miles per Gallon _____

Gas Station or Brand _____

_____

Date _____ Mileage_____

Fuel Amount Added _____

Price per Gallon _____

Miles per Gallon _____

Gas Station or Brand _____

_____

Date _____ Mileage_____

Fuel Amount Added _____

Price per Gallon _____

Miles per Gallon _____

Gas Station or Brand _____

_____

Date _____ Mileage_____
Fuel Amount Added _____
Price per Gallon _____
Miles per Gallon _____
Gas Station or Brand _____

_____

Date _____ Mileage_____
Fuel Amount Added _____
Price per Gallon _____
Miles per Gallon _____
Gas Station or Brand _____

_____

Date _____ Mileage_____
Fuel Amount Added _____
Price per Gallon _____
Miles per Gallon _____
Gas Station or Brand _____

_____

Fuel Stops

Date _____ Mileage_____
Fuel Amount Added _____
Price per Gallon _____
Miles per Gallon _____
Gas Station or Brand _____

_____

Date _____ Mileage_____
Fuel Amount Added _____
Price per Gallon _____
Miles per Gallon _____
Gas Station or Brand _____

_____

Date _____ Mileage_____
Fuel Amount Added _____
Price per Gallon _____
Miles per Gallon _____
Gas Station or Brand _____

_____

Date _____ Mileage_____

Fuel Amount Added _____

Price per Gallon _____

Miles per Gallon _____

Gas Station or Brand _____

_____

Date _____ Mileage_____

Fuel Amount Added _____

Price per Gallon _____

Miles per Gallon _____

Gas Station or Brand _____

_____

Date _____ Mileage_____

Fuel Amount Added _____

Price per Gallon _____

Miles per Gallon _____

Gas Station or Brand _____

_____

Fuel Stops

Date _____ Mileage_____
Fuel Amount Added _____
Price per Gallon _____
Miles per Gallon _____
Gas Station or Brand _____

_____

Date _____ Mileage_____
Fuel Amount Added _____
Price per Gallon _____
Miles per Gallon _____
Gas Station or Brand _____

_____

Date _____ Mileage_____
Fuel Amount Added _____
Price per Gallon _____
Miles per Gallon _____
Gas Station or Brand _____

_____

Date _____ Mileage_____
Fuel Amount Added _____
Price per Gallon _____
Miles per Gallon _____
Gas Station or Brand _____

_____

Date _____ Mileage_____
Fuel Amount Added _____
Price per Gallon _____
Miles per Gallon _____
Gas Station or Brand _____

_____

Date _____ Mileage_____
Fuel Amount Added _____
Price per Gallon _____
Miles per Gallon _____
Gas Station or Brand _____

_____

Fuel Stops

Date _____ Mileage_____
Fuel Amount Added _____
Price per Gallon _____
Miles per Gallon _____
Gas Station or Brand _____

_____

Date _____ Mileage_____
Fuel Amount Added _____
Price per Gallon _____
Miles per Gallon _____
Gas Station or Brand _____

_____

Date _____ Mileage_____
Fuel Amount Added _____
Price per Gallon _____
Miles per Gallon _____
Gas Station or Brand _____

_____

Fuel Stops

Date _____ Mileage_____
Fuel Amount Added _____
Price per Gallon _____
Miles per Gallon _____
Gas Station or Brand _____

_____

Date _____ Mileage_____
Fuel Amount Added _____
Price per Gallon _____
Miles per Gallon _____
Gas Station or Brand _____

_____

Date _____ Mileage_____
Fuel Amount Added _____
Price per Gallon _____
Miles per Gallon _____
Gas Station or Brand _____

_____

Date _____ Mileage_____
Fuel Amount Added _____
Price per Gallon _____
Miles per Gallon _____
Gas Station or Brand _____

_____

Date _____ Mileage_____
Fuel Amount Added _____
Price per Gallon _____
Miles per Gallon _____
Gas Station or Brand _____

_____

Date _____ Mileage_____
Fuel Amount Added _____
Price per Gallon _____
Miles per Gallon _____
Gas Station or Brand _____

_____

Fuel Stops

Date _____ Mileage_____
Fuel Amount Added _____
Price per Gallon _____
Miles per Gallon _____
Gas Station or Brand _____

_____

Date _____ Mileage_____
Fuel Amount Added _____
Price per Gallon _____
Miles per Gallon _____
Gas Station or Brand _____

_____

Date _____ Mileage_____
Fuel Amount Added _____
Price per Gallon _____
Miles per Gallon _____
Gas Station or Brand _____

_____

Fuel Stops

Date _____ Mileage_____
Fuel Amount Added _____
Price per Gallon _____
Miles per Gallon _____
Gas Station or Brand _____

_____

Date _____ Mileage_____
Fuel Amount Added _____
Price per Gallon _____
Miles per Gallon _____
Gas Station or Brand _____

_____

Date _____ Mileage_____
Fuel Amount Added _____
Price per Gallon _____
Miles per Gallon _____
Gas Station or Brand _____

_____

Date _____ Mileage_____
Fuel Amount Added _____
Price per Gallon _____
Miles per Gallon _____
Gas Station or Brand _____

_____

Date _____ Mileage_____
Fuel Amount Added _____
Price per Gallon _____
Miles per Gallon _____
Gas Station or Brand _____

_____

Date _____ Mileage_____
Fuel Amount Added _____
Price per Gallon _____
Miles per Gallon _____
Gas Station or Brand _____

_____

Fuel Stops

Date _____ Mileage_____
Fuel Amount Added _____
Price per Gallon _____
Miles per Gallon _____
Gas Station or Brand _____

_____

Date _____ Mileage_____
Fuel Amount Added _____
Price per Gallon _____
Miles per Gallon _____
Gas Station or Brand _____

_____

Date _____ Mileage_____
Fuel Amount Added _____
Price per Gallon _____
Miles per Gallon _____
Gas Station or Brand _____

_____

Date _____ Mileage_____
Fuel Amount Added _____
Price per Gallon _____
Miles per Gallon _____
Gas Station or Brand _____

_____

Date _____ Mileage_____
Fuel Amount Added _____
Price per Gallon _____
Miles per Gallon _____
Gas Station or Brand _____

_____

Date _____ Mileage_____
Fuel Amount Added _____
Price per Gallon _____
Miles per Gallon _____
Gas Station or Brand _____

_____

Fuel Stops

Date _____ Mileage_____
Fuel Amount Added _____
Price per Gallon _____
Miles per Gallon _____
Gas Station or Brand _____

_____

Date _____ Mileage_____
Fuel Amount Added _____
Price per Gallon _____
Miles per Gallon _____
Gas Station or Brand _____

_____

Date _____ Mileage_____
Fuel Amount Added _____
Price per Gallon _____
Miles per Gallon _____
Gas Station or Brand _____

_____

Date _____ Mileage_____
Fuel Amount Added _____
Price per Gallon _____
Miles per Gallon _____
Gas Station or Brand _____

_____

Date _____ Mileage_____
Fuel Amount Added _____
Price per Gallon _____
Miles per Gallon _____
Gas Station or Brand _____

_____

Date _____ Mileage_____
Fuel Amount Added _____
Price per Gallon _____
Miles per Gallon _____
Gas Station or Brand _____

_____

Date _____ Mileage_____
Fuel Amount Added _____
Price per Gallon _____
Miles per Gallon _____
Gas Station or Brand _____

_____

Date _____ Mileage_____
Fuel Amount Added _____
Price per Gallon _____
Miles per Gallon _____
Gas Station or Brand _____

_____

Date _____ Mileage_____
Fuel Amount Added _____
Price per Gallon _____
Miles per Gallon _____
Gas Station or Brand _____

_____

Fuel Stops

Date _____ Mileage_____
Fuel Amount Added _____
Price per Gallon _____
Miles per Gallon _____
Gas Station or Brand _____

_____

Date _____ Mileage_____
Fuel Amount Added _____
Price per Gallon _____
Miles per Gallon _____
Gas Station or Brand _____

_____

Date _____ Mileage_____
Fuel Amount Added _____
Price per Gallon _____
Miles per Gallon _____
Gas Station or Brand _____

_____

Fuel Stops

Date _____ Mileage_____
Fuel Amount Added _____
Price per Gallon _____
Miles per Gallon _____
Gas Station or Brand _____

_____

Date _____ Mileage_____
Fuel Amount Added _____
Price per Gallon _____
Miles per Gallon _____
Gas Station or Brand _____

_____

Date _____ Mileage_____
Fuel Amount Added _____
Price per Gallon _____
Miles per Gallon _____
Gas Station or Brand _____

_____

Fuel Stops

Date _____ Mileage_____
Fuel Amount Added _____
Price per Gallon _____
Miles per Gallon _____
Gas Station or Brand _____

_____

Date _____ Mileage_____
Fuel Amount Added _____
Price per Gallon _____
Miles per Gallon _____
Gas Station or Brand _____

_____

Date _____ Mileage_____
Fuel Amount Added _____
Price per Gallon _____
Miles per Gallon _____
Gas Station or Brand _____

_____

Fuel Stops

Date _____ Mileage_____
Fuel Amount Added _____
Price per Gallon _____
Miles per Gallon _____
Gas Station or Brand _____

_____

Date _____ Mileage_____
Fuel Amount Added _____
Price per Gallon _____
Miles per Gallon _____
Gas Station or Brand _____

_____

Date _____ Mileage_____
Fuel Amount Added _____
Price per Gallon _____
Miles per Gallon _____
Gas Station or Brand _____

_____

Date _____ Mileage_____
Fuel Amount Added _____
Price per Gallon _____
Miles per Gallon _____
Gas Station or Brand _____

_____

Date _____ Mileage_____
Fuel Amount Added _____
Price per Gallon _____
Miles per Gallon _____
Gas Station or Brand _____

_____

Date _____ Mileage_____
Fuel Amount Added _____
Price per Gallon _____
Miles per Gallon _____
Gas Station or Brand _____

_____

Fuel Stops

Date _____ Mileage_____

Fuel Amount Added _____

Price per Gallon _____

Miles per Gallon _____

Gas Station or Brand _____

_____

Date _____ Mileage_____

Fuel Amount Added _____

Price per Gallon _____

Miles per Gallon _____

Gas Station or Brand _____

_____

Date _____ Mileage_____

Fuel Amount Added _____

Price per Gallon _____

Miles per Gallon _____

Gas Station or Brand _____

_____

Date _____ Mileage_____
Fuel Amount Added _____
Price per Gallon _____
Miles per Gallon _____
Gas Station or Brand _____

_____

Date _____ Mileage_____
Fuel Amount Added _____
Price per Gallon _____
Miles per Gallon _____
Gas Station or Brand _____

_____

Date _____ Mileage_____
Fuel Amount Added _____
Price per Gallon _____
Miles per Gallon _____
Gas Station or Brand _____

_____

Fuel Stops

Date _____ Mileage_____

Fuel Amount Added _____

Price per Gallon _____

Miles per Gallon _____

Gas Station or Brand _____

_____

Date _____ Mileage_____

Fuel Amount Added _____

Price per Gallon _____

Miles per Gallon _____

Gas Station or Brand _____

_____

Date _____ Mileage_____

Fuel Amount Added _____

Price per Gallon _____

Miles per Gallon _____

Gas Station or Brand _____

_____

Date _____ Mileage_____
Fuel Amount Added _____
Price per Gallon _____
Miles per Gallon _____
Gas Station or Brand _____

_____

Date _____ Mileage_____
Fuel Amount Added _____
Price per Gallon _____
Miles per Gallon _____
Gas Station or Brand _____

_____

Date _____ Mileage_____
Fuel Amount Added _____
Price per Gallon _____
Miles per Gallon _____
Gas Station or Brand _____

_____

Fuel Stops

Date _____ Mileage_____
Fuel Amount Added _____
Price per Gallon _____
Miles per Gallon _____
Gas Station or Brand _____

_____

Date _____ Mileage_____
Fuel Amount Added _____
Price per Gallon _____
Miles per Gallon _____
Gas Station or Brand _____

_____

Date _____ Mileage_____
Fuel Amount Added _____
Price per Gallon _____
Miles per Gallon _____
Gas Station or Brand _____

_____

Date _____ Mileage_____
Fuel Amount Added _____
Price per Gallon _____
Miles per Gallon _____
Gas Station or Brand _____

_____

Date _____ Mileage_____
Fuel Amount Added _____
Price per Gallon _____
Miles per Gallon _____
Gas Station or Brand _____

_____

Date _____ Mileage_____
Fuel Amount Added _____
Price per Gallon _____
Miles per Gallon _____
Gas Station or Brand _____

_____

Fuel Stops

Date _____ Mileage_____
Fuel Amount Added _____
Price per Gallon _____
Miles per Gallon _____
Gas Station or Brand _____

_____

Date _____ Mileage_____
Fuel Amount Added _____
Price per Gallon _____
Miles per Gallon _____
Gas Station or Brand _____

_____

Date _____ Mileage_____
Fuel Amount Added _____
Price per Gallon _____
Miles per Gallon _____
Gas Station or Brand _____

_____

Date _____ Mileage_____
Fuel Amount Added _____
Price per Gallon _____
Miles per Gallon _____
Gas Station or Brand _____

_____

Date _____ Mileage_____
Fuel Amount Added _____
Price per Gallon _____
Miles per Gallon _____
Gas Station or Brand _____

_____

Date _____ Mileage_____
Fuel Amount Added _____
Price per Gallon _____
Miles per Gallon _____
Gas Station or Brand _____

_____

Date _____ Mileage_____
Fuel Amount Added _____
Price per Gallon _____
Miles per Gallon _____
Gas Station or Brand _____

_____

Date _____ Mileage_____
Fuel Amount Added _____
Price per Gallon _____
Miles per Gallon _____
Gas Station or Brand _____

_____

Date _____ Mileage_____
Fuel Amount Added _____
Price per Gallon _____
Miles per Gallon _____
Gas Station or Brand _____

_____

Date _____ Mileage_____
Fuel Amount Added _____
Price per Gallon _____
Miles per Gallon _____
Gas Station or Brand _____

_____

Date _____ Mileage_____
Fuel Amount Added _____
Price per Gallon _____
Miles per Gallon _____
Gas Station or Brand _____

_____

Date _____ Mileage_____
Fuel Amount Added _____
Price per Gallon _____
Miles per Gallon _____
Gas Station or Brand _____

_____

Fuel Stops

Date _____ Mileage_____
Fuel Amount Added _____
Price per Gallon _____
Miles per Gallon _____
Gas Station or Brand _____

_____

Date _____ Mileage_____
Fuel Amount Added _____
Price per Gallon _____
Miles per Gallon _____
Gas Station or Brand _____

_____

Date _____ Mileage_____
Fuel Amount Added _____
Price per Gallon _____
Miles per Gallon _____
Gas Station or Brand _____

_____

Date _____ Mileage_____
Fuel Amount Added _____
Price per Gallon _____
Miles per Gallon _____
Gas Station or Brand _____

_____

Date _____ Mileage_____
Fuel Amount Added _____
Price per Gallon _____
Miles per Gallon _____
Gas Station or Brand _____

_____

Date _____ Mileage_____
Fuel Amount Added _____
Price per Gallon _____
Miles per Gallon _____
Gas Station or Brand _____

_____

Fuel Stops

Date _____ Mileage_____

Fuel Amount Added _____

Price per Gallon _____

Miles per Gallon _____

Gas Station or Brand _____

_____

Date _____ Mileage_____

Fuel Amount Added _____

Price per Gallon _____

Miles per Gallon _____

Gas Station or Brand _____

_____

Date _____ Mileage_____

Fuel Amount Added _____

Price per Gallon _____

Miles per Gallon _____

Gas Station or Brand _____

_____

Date _____ Mileage_____
Fuel Amount Added _____
Price per Gallon _____
Miles per Gallon _____
Gas Station or Brand _____

_____

Date _____ Mileage_____
Fuel Amount Added _____
Price per Gallon _____
Miles per Gallon _____
Gas Station or Brand _____

_____

Date _____ Mileage_____
Fuel Amount Added _____
Price per Gallon _____
Miles per Gallon _____
Gas Station or Brand _____

_____

Fuel Stops

Date _____ Mileage_____
Fuel Amount Added _____
Price per Gallon _____
Miles per Gallon _____
Gas Station or Brand _____

_____

Date _____ Mileage_____
Fuel Amount Added _____
Price per Gallon _____
Miles per Gallon _____
Gas Station or Brand _____

_____

Date _____ Mileage_____
Fuel Amount Added _____
Price per Gallon _____
Miles per Gallon _____
Gas Station or Brand _____

_____

Date _____ Mileage_____
Fuel Amount Added _____
Price per Gallon _____
Miles per Gallon _____
Gas Station or Brand _____

_____

Date _____ Mileage_____
Fuel Amount Added _____
Price per Gallon _____
Miles per Gallon _____
Gas Station or Brand _____

_____

Date _____ Mileage_____
Fuel Amount Added _____
Price per Gallon _____
Miles per Gallon _____
Gas Station or Brand _____

_____

Fuel Stops

Date _____ Mileage_____
Fuel Amount Added _____
Price per Gallon _____
Miles per Gallon _____
Gas Station or Brand _____

_____

Date _____ Mileage_____
Fuel Amount Added _____
Price per Gallon _____
Miles per Gallon _____
Gas Station or Brand _____

_____

Date _____ Mileage_____
Fuel Amount Added _____
Price per Gallon _____
Miles per Gallon _____
Gas Station or Brand _____

_____

Fuel Stops

Date _____ Mileage_____

Fuel Amount Added _____

Price per Gallon _____

Miles per Gallon _____

Gas Station or Brand _____

_____

Date _____ Mileage_____

Fuel Amount Added _____

Price per Gallon _____

Miles per Gallon _____

Gas Station or Brand _____

_____

Date _____ Mileage_____

Fuel Amount Added _____

Price per Gallon _____

Miles per Gallon _____

Gas Station or Brand _____

_____

Fuel Stops

Date _____ Mileage_____
Fuel Amount Added _____
Price per Gallon _____
Miles per Gallon _____
Gas Station or Brand _____

_____

Date _____ Mileage_____
Fuel Amount Added _____
Price per Gallon _____
Miles per Gallon _____
Gas Station or Brand _____

_____

Date _____ Mileage_____
Fuel Amount Added _____
Price per Gallon _____
Miles per Gallon _____
Gas Station or Brand _____

_____

Date _____ Mileage_____
Fuel Amount Added _____
Price per Gallon _____
Miles per Gallon _____
Gas Station or Brand _____

_____

Date _____ Mileage_____
Fuel Amount Added _____
Price per Gallon _____
Miles per Gallon _____
Gas Station or Brand _____

_____

Date _____ Mileage_____
Fuel Amount Added _____
Price per Gallon _____
Miles per Gallon _____
Gas Station or Brand _____

_____

Fuel Stops

Date _____ Mileage_____
Fuel Amount Added _____
Price per Gallon _____
Miles per Gallon _____
Gas Station or Brand _____

_____

Date _____ Mileage_____
Fuel Amount Added _____
Price per Gallon _____
Miles per Gallon _____
Gas Station or Brand _____

_____

Date _____ Mileage_____
Fuel Amount Added _____
Price per Gallon _____
Miles per Gallon _____
Gas Station or Brand _____

_____

Date _____ Mileage_____
Fuel Amount Added _____
Price per Gallon _____
Miles per Gallon _____
Gas Station or Brand _____

_____

Date _____ Mileage_____
Fuel Amount Added _____
Price per Gallon _____
Miles per Gallon _____
Gas Station or Brand _____

_____

Date _____ Mileage_____
Fuel Amount Added _____
Price per Gallon _____
Miles per Gallon _____
Gas Station or Brand _____

_____

Fuel Stops

Date _____ Mileage_____
Fuel Amount Added _____
Price per Gallon _____
Miles per Gallon _____
Gas Station or Brand _____

_____

Date _____ Mileage_____
Fuel Amount Added _____
Price per Gallon _____
Miles per Gallon _____
Gas Station or Brand _____

_____

Date _____ Mileage_____
Fuel Amount Added _____
Price per Gallon _____
Miles per Gallon _____
Gas Station or Brand _____

_____

Date _____ Mileage_____
Fuel Amount Added _____
Price per Gallon _____
Miles per Gallon _____
Gas Station or Brand _____

_____

Date _____ Mileage_____
Fuel Amount Added _____
Price per Gallon _____
Miles per Gallon _____
Gas Station or Brand _____

_____

Date _____ Mileage_____
Fuel Amount Added _____
Price per Gallon _____
Miles per Gallon _____
Gas Station or Brand _____

_____

Fuel Stops

Date _____ Mileage_____

Fuel Amount Added _____

Price per Gallon _____

Miles per Gallon _____

Gas Station or Brand _____

_____

Date _____ Mileage_____

Fuel Amount Added _____

Price per Gallon _____

Miles per Gallon _____

Gas Station or Brand _____

_____

Date _____ Mileage_____

Fuel Amount Added _____

Price per Gallon _____

Miles per Gallon _____

Gas Station or Brand _____

_____

Date _____ Mileage_____
Fuel Amount Added _____
Price per Gallon _____
Miles per Gallon _____
Gas Station or Brand _____

_____

Date _____ Mileage_____
Fuel Amount Added _____
Price per Gallon _____
Miles per Gallon _____
Gas Station or Brand _____

_____

Date _____ Mileage_____
Fuel Amount Added _____
Price per Gallon _____
Miles per Gallon _____
Gas Station or Brand _____

_____

Date _____ Mileage_____
Fuel Amount Added _____
Price per Gallon _____
Miles per Gallon _____
Gas Station or Brand _____

_____

Date _____ Mileage_____
Fuel Amount Added _____
Price per Gallon _____
Miles per Gallon _____
Gas Station or Brand _____

_____

Date _____ Mileage_____
Fuel Amount Added _____
Price per Gallon _____
Miles per Gallon _____
Gas Station or Brand _____

_____

Date _____ Mileage_____
Fuel Amount Added _____
Price per Gallon _____
Miles per Gallon _____
Gas Station or Brand _____

_____

Date _____ Mileage_____
Fuel Amount Added _____
Price per Gallon _____
Miles per Gallon _____
Gas Station or Brand _____

_____

Date _____ Mileage_____
Fuel Amount Added _____
Price per Gallon _____
Miles per Gallon _____
Gas Station or Brand _____

_____

Fuel Stops

Date _____ Mileage_____
Fuel Amount Added _____
Price per Gallon _____
Miles per Gallon _____
Gas Station or Brand _____

_____

Date _____ Mileage_____
Fuel Amount Added _____
Price per Gallon _____
Miles per Gallon _____
Gas Station or Brand _____

_____

Date _____ Mileage_____
Fuel Amount Added _____
Price per Gallon _____
Miles per Gallon _____
Gas Station or Brand _____

_____

Date _____ Mileage_____
Fuel Amount Added _____
Price per Gallon _____
Miles per Gallon _____
Gas Station or Brand _____

_____

Date _____ Mileage_____
Fuel Amount Added _____
Price per Gallon _____
Miles per Gallon _____
Gas Station or Brand _____

_____

Date _____ Mileage_____
Fuel Amount Added _____
Price per Gallon _____
Miles per Gallon _____
Gas Station or Brand _____

_____

Date _____ Mileage_____
Fuel Amount Added _____
Price per Gallon _____
Miles per Gallon _____
Gas Station or Brand _____

_____

Date _____ Mileage_____
Fuel Amount Added _____
Price per Gallon _____
Miles per Gallon _____
Gas Station or Brand _____

_____

Date _____ Mileage_____
Fuel Amount Added _____
Price per Gallon _____
Miles per Gallon _____
Gas Station or Brand _____

_____

Date _____ Mileage_____
Fuel Amount Added _____
Price per Gallon _____
Miles per Gallon _____
Gas Station or Brand _____

_____

Date _____ Mileage_____
Fuel Amount Added _____
Price per Gallon _____
Miles per Gallon _____
Gas Station or Brand _____

_____

Date _____ Mileage_____
Fuel Amount Added _____
Price per Gallon _____
Miles per Gallon _____
Gas Station or Brand _____

_____

Fuel Stops

Date _____ Mileage_____
Fuel Amount Added _____
Price per Gallon _____
Miles per Gallon _____
Gas Station or Brand _____

_____

Date _____ Mileage_____
Fuel Amount Added _____
Price per Gallon _____
Miles per Gallon _____
Gas Station or Brand _____

_____

Date _____ Mileage_____
Fuel Amount Added _____
Price per Gallon _____
Miles per Gallon _____
Gas Station or Brand _____

_____

Date _____ Mileage_____
Fuel Amount Added _____
Price per Gallon _____
Miles per Gallon _____
Gas Station or Brand _____

_____

Date _____ Mileage_____
Fuel Amount Added _____
Price per Gallon _____
Miles per Gallon _____
Gas Station or Brand _____

_____

Date _____ Mileage_____
Fuel Amount Added _____
Price per Gallon _____
Miles per Gallon _____
Gas Station or Brand _____

_____

Fuel Stops

Date _____ Mileage_____
Fuel Amount Added _____
Price per Gallon _____
Miles per Gallon _____
Gas Station or Brand _____

_____

Date _____ Mileage_____
Fuel Amount Added _____
Price per Gallon _____
Miles per Gallon _____
Gas Station or Brand _____

_____

Date _____ Mileage_____
Fuel Amount Added _____
Price per Gallon _____
Miles per Gallon _____
Gas Station or Brand _____

_____

Date _____ Mileage_____
Fuel Amount Added _____
Price per Gallon _____
Miles per Gallon _____
Gas Station or Brand _____

_____

Date _____ Mileage_____
Fuel Amount Added _____
Price per Gallon _____
Miles per Gallon _____
Gas Station or Brand _____

_____

Date _____ Mileage_____
Fuel Amount Added _____
Price per Gallon _____
Miles per Gallon _____
Gas Station or Brand _____

_____

Date _____ Mileage_____
Fuel Amount Added _____
Price per Gallon _____
Miles per Gallon _____
Gas Station or Brand _____

_____

Date _____ Mileage_____
Fuel Amount Added _____
Price per Gallon _____
Miles per Gallon _____
Gas Station or Brand _____

_____

Date _____ Mileage_____
Fuel Amount Added _____
Price per Gallon _____
Miles per Gallon _____
Gas Station or Brand _____

_____

Date _____ Mileage_____

Fuel Amount Added _____

Price per Gallon _____

Miles per Gallon _____

Gas Station or Brand _____

_____

Date _____ Mileage_____

Fuel Amount Added _____

Price per Gallon _____

Miles per Gallon _____

Gas Station or Brand _____

_____

Date _____ Mileage_____

Fuel Amount Added _____

Price per Gallon _____

Miles per Gallon _____

Gas Station or Brand _____

_____

Fuel Stops

Date _____ Mileage_____
Fuel Amount Added _____
Price per Gallon _____
Miles per Gallon _____
Gas Station or Brand _____

_____

Date _____ Mileage_____
Fuel Amount Added _____
Price per Gallon _____
Miles per Gallon _____
Gas Station or Brand _____

_____

Date _____ Mileage_____
Fuel Amount Added _____
Price per Gallon _____
Miles per Gallon _____
Gas Station or Brand _____

_____

Date _____ Mileage_____
Fuel Amount Added _____
Price per Gallon _____
Miles per Gallon _____
Gas Station or Brand _____

_____

Date _____ Mileage_____
Fuel Amount Added _____
Price per Gallon _____
Miles per Gallon _____
Gas Station or Brand _____

_____

Date _____ Mileage_____
Fuel Amount Added _____
Price per Gallon _____
Miles per Gallon _____
Gas Station or Brand _____

_____

Date _____ Mileage_____
Fuel Amount Added _____
Price per Gallon _____
Miles per Gallon _____
Gas Station or Brand _____

_____

Date _____ Mileage_____
Fuel Amount Added _____
Price per Gallon _____
Miles per Gallon _____
Gas Station or Brand _____

_____

Date _____ Mileage_____
Fuel Amount Added _____
Price per Gallon _____
Miles per Gallon _____
Gas Station or Brand _____

_____

Date _____ Mileage_____
Fuel Amount Added _____
Price per Gallon _____
Miles per Gallon _____
Gas Station or Brand _____

_____

Date _____ Mileage_____
Fuel Amount Added _____
Price per Gallon _____
Miles per Gallon _____
Gas Station or Brand _____

_____

Date _____ Mileage_____
Fuel Amount Added _____
Price per Gallon _____
Miles per Gallon _____
Gas Station or Brand _____

_____

Fuel Stops

Date _____ Mileage_____
Fuel Amount Added _____
Price per Gallon _____
Miles per Gallon _____
Gas Station or Brand _____

_____

Date _____ Mileage_____
Fuel Amount Added _____
Price per Gallon _____
Miles per Gallon _____
Gas Station or Brand _____

_____

Date _____ Mileage_____
Fuel Amount Added _____
Price per Gallon _____
Miles per Gallon _____
Gas Station or Brand _____

_____

Date _____ Mileage_____
Fuel Amount Added _____
Price per Gallon _____
Miles per Gallon _____
Gas Station or Brand _____

_____

Date _____ Mileage_____
Fuel Amount Added _____
Price per Gallon _____
Miles per Gallon _____
Gas Station or Brand _____

_____

Date _____ Mileage_____
Fuel Amount Added _____
Price per Gallon _____
Miles per Gallon _____
Gas Station or Brand _____

_____

Date _____ Mileage_____
Fuel Amount Added _____
Price per Gallon _____
Miles per Gallon _____
Gas Station or Brand _____

_____

Date _____ Mileage_____
Fuel Amount Added _____
Price per Gallon _____
Miles per Gallon _____
Gas Station or Brand _____

_____

Date _____ Mileage_____
Fuel Amount Added _____
Price per Gallon _____
Miles per Gallon _____
Gas Station or Brand _____

_____

Date _____ Mileage_____
Fuel Amount Added _____
Price per Gallon _____
Miles per Gallon _____
Gas Station or Brand _____

_____

Date _____ Mileage_____
Fuel Amount Added _____
Price per Gallon _____
Miles per Gallon _____
Gas Station or Brand _____

_____

Date _____ Mileage_____
Fuel Amount Added _____
Price per Gallon _____
Miles per Gallon _____
Gas Station or Brand _____

_____

Fuel Stops

Date _____ Mileage_____
Fuel Amount Added _____
Price per Gallon _____
Miles per Gallon _____
Gas Station or Brand _____

_____

Date _____ Mileage_____
Fuel Amount Added _____
Price per Gallon _____
Miles per Gallon _____
Gas Station or Brand _____

_____

Date _____ Mileage_____
Fuel Amount Added _____
Price per Gallon _____
Miles per Gallon _____
Gas Station or Brand _____

_____

Date _____ Mileage_____
Fuel Amount Added _____
Price per Gallon _____
Miles per Gallon _____
Gas Station or Brand _____

_____

Date _____ Mileage_____
Fuel Amount Added _____
Price per Gallon _____
Miles per Gallon _____
Gas Station or Brand _____

_____

Date _____ Mileage_____
Fuel Amount Added _____
Price per Gallon _____
Miles per Gallon _____
Gas Station or Brand _____

_____

Fuel Stops

Date _____ Mileage_____
Fuel Amount Added _____
Price per Gallon _____
Miles per Gallon _____
Gas Station or Brand _____

_____

Date _____ Mileage_____
Fuel Amount Added _____
Price per Gallon _____
Miles per Gallon _____
Gas Station or Brand _____

_____

Date _____ Mileage_____
Fuel Amount Added _____
Price per Gallon _____
Miles per Gallon _____
Gas Station or Brand _____

_____

Date _____ Mileage_____
Fuel Amount Added _____
Price per Gallon _____
Miles per Gallon _____
Gas Station or Brand _____

_____

Date _____ Mileage_____
Fuel Amount Added _____
Price per Gallon _____
Miles per Gallon _____
Gas Station or Brand _____

_____

Date _____ Mileage_____
Fuel Amount Added _____
Price per Gallon _____
Miles per Gallon _____
Gas Station or Brand _____

_____

Fuel Stops

Date _____ Mileage_____
Fuel Amount Added _____
Price per Gallon _____
Miles per Gallon _____
Gas Station or Brand _____

_____

Date _____ Mileage_____
Fuel Amount Added _____
Price per Gallon _____
Miles per Gallon _____
Gas Station or Brand _____

_____

Date _____ Mileage_____
Fuel Amount Added _____
Price per Gallon _____
Miles per Gallon _____
Gas Station or Brand _____

_____

Date _____ Mileage_____
Fuel Amount Added _____
Price per Gallon _____
Miles per Gallon _____
Gas Station or Brand _____

_____

Date _____ Mileage_____
Fuel Amount Added _____
Price per Gallon _____
Miles per Gallon _____
Gas Station or Brand _____

_____

Date _____ Mileage_____
Fuel Amount Added _____
Price per Gallon _____
Miles per Gallon _____
Gas Station or Brand _____

_____

Date _____ Mileage_____
Fuel Amount Added _____
Price per Gallon _____
Miles per Gallon _____
Gas Station or Brand _____

_____

Date _____ Mileage_____
Fuel Amount Added _____
Price per Gallon _____
Miles per Gallon _____
Gas Station or Brand _____

_____

Date _____ Mileage_____
Fuel Amount Added _____
Price per Gallon _____
Miles per Gallon _____
Gas Station or Brand _____

_____

Date _____ Mileage_____
Fuel Amount Added _____
Price per Gallon _____
Miles per Gallon _____
Gas Station or Brand _____

_____

Date _____ Mileage_____
Fuel Amount Added _____
Price per Gallon _____
Miles per Gallon _____
Gas Station or Brand _____

_____

Date _____ Mileage_____
Fuel Amount Added _____
Price per Gallon _____
Miles per Gallon _____
Gas Station or Brand _____

_____

Date _____ Mileage_____
Fuel Amount Added _____
Price per Gallon _____
Miles per Gallon _____
Gas Station or Brand _____

_____

Date _____ Mileage_____
Fuel Amount Added _____
Price per Gallon _____
Miles per Gallon _____
Gas Station or Brand _____

_____

Date _____ Mileage_____
Fuel Amount Added _____
Price per Gallon _____
Miles per Gallon _____
Gas Station or Brand _____

_____

Date _____ Mileage_____
Fuel Amount Added _____
Price per Gallon _____
Miles per Gallon _____
Gas Station or Brand _____

_____

Date _____ Mileage_____
Fuel Amount Added _____
Price per Gallon _____
Miles per Gallon _____
Gas Station or Brand _____

_____

Date _____ Mileage_____
Fuel Amount Added _____
Price per Gallon _____
Miles per Gallon _____
Gas Station or Brand _____

_____

Fuel Stops

Date _____ Mileage_____
Fuel Amount Added _____
Price per Gallon _____
Miles per Gallon _____
Gas Station or Brand _____

_____

Date _____ Mileage_____
Fuel Amount Added _____
Price per Gallon _____
Miles per Gallon _____
Gas Station or Brand _____

_____

Date _____ Mileage_____
Fuel Amount Added _____
Price per Gallon _____
Miles per Gallon _____
Gas Station or Brand _____

_____

Date _____ Mileage_____
Fuel Amount Added _____
Price per Gallon _____
Miles per Gallon _____
Gas Station or Brand _____

_____

Date _____ Mileage_____
Fuel Amount Added _____
Price per Gallon _____
Miles per Gallon _____
Gas Station or Brand _____

_____

Date _____ Mileage_____
Fuel Amount Added _____
Price per Gallon _____
Miles per Gallon _____
Gas Station or Brand _____

_____

Fuel Stops

Date _____ Mileage_____
Fuel Amount Added _____
Price per Gallon _____
Miles per Gallon _____
Gas Station or Brand _____

_____

Date _____ Mileage_____
Fuel Amount Added _____
Price per Gallon _____
Miles per Gallon _____
Gas Station or Brand _____

_____

Date _____ Mileage_____
Fuel Amount Added _____
Price per Gallon _____
Miles per Gallon _____
Gas Station or Brand _____

_____

Date _____ Mileage_____
Fuel Amount Added _____
Price per Gallon _____
Miles per Gallon _____
Gas Station or Brand _____

_____

Date _____ Mileage_____
Fuel Amount Added _____
Price per Gallon _____
Miles per Gallon _____
Gas Station or Brand _____

_____

Date _____ Mileage_____
Fuel Amount Added _____
Price per Gallon _____
Miles per Gallon _____
Gas Station or Brand _____

_____

Fuel Stops

Date _____ Mileage_____
Fuel Amount Added _____
Price per Gallon _____
Miles per Gallon _____
Gas Station or Brand _____

_____

Date _____ Mileage_____
Fuel Amount Added _____
Price per Gallon _____
Miles per Gallon _____
Gas Station or Brand _____

_____

Date _____ Mileage_____
Fuel Amount Added _____
Price per Gallon _____
Miles per Gallon _____
Gas Station or Brand _____

_____

Date _____ Mileage_____
Fuel Amount Added _____
Price per Gallon _____
Miles per Gallon _____
Gas Station or Brand _____

_____

Date _____ Mileage_____
Fuel Amount Added _____
Price per Gallon _____
Miles per Gallon _____
Gas Station or Brand _____

_____

Date _____ Mileage_____
Fuel Amount Added _____
Price per Gallon _____
Miles per Gallon _____
Gas Station or Brand _____

_____

Fuel Stops

Date _____ Mileage_____
Fuel Amount Added _____
Price per Gallon _____
Miles per Gallon _____
Gas Station or Brand _____

_____

Date _____ Mileage_____
Fuel Amount Added _____
Price per Gallon _____
Miles per Gallon _____
Gas Station or Brand _____

_____

Date _____ Mileage_____
Fuel Amount Added _____
Price per Gallon _____
Miles per Gallon _____
Gas Station or Brand _____

_____

Fuel Stops

Date _____ Mileage_____
Fuel Amount Added _____
Price per Gallon _____
Miles per Gallon _____
Gas Station or Brand _____

_____

Date _____ Mileage_____
Fuel Amount Added _____
Price per Gallon _____
Miles per Gallon _____
Gas Station or Brand _____

_____

Date _____ Mileage_____
Fuel Amount Added _____
Price per Gallon _____
Miles per Gallon _____
Gas Station or Brand _____

_____

Date _____ Mileage_____

Fuel Amount Added _____

Price per Gallon _____

Miles per Gallon _____

Gas Station or Brand _____

_____

Date _____ Mileage_____

Fuel Amount Added _____

Price per Gallon _____

Miles per Gallon _____

Gas Station or Brand _____

_____

Date _____ Mileage_____

Fuel Amount Added _____

Price per Gallon _____

Miles per Gallon _____

Gas Station or Brand _____

_____

Date _____ Mileage_____
Fuel Amount Added _____
Price per Gallon _____
Miles per Gallon _____
Gas Station or Brand _____

_____

Date _____ Mileage_____
Fuel Amount Added _____
Price per Gallon _____
Miles per Gallon _____
Gas Station or Brand _____

_____

Date _____ Mileage_____
Fuel Amount Added _____
Price per Gallon _____
Miles per Gallon _____
Gas Station or Brand _____

_____

Date _____ Mileage_____
Fuel Amount Added _____
Price per Gallon _____
Miles per Gallon _____
Gas Station or Brand _____

_____

Date _____ Mileage_____
Fuel Amount Added _____
Price per Gallon _____
Miles per Gallon _____
Gas Station or Brand _____

_____

Date _____ Mileage_____
Fuel Amount Added _____
Price per Gallon _____
Miles per Gallon _____
Gas Station or Brand _____

_____

Fuel Stops

Date _____ Mileage_____
Fuel Amount Added _____
Price per Gallon _____
Miles per Gallon _____
Gas Station or Brand _____

_____

Date _____ Mileage_____
Fuel Amount Added _____
Price per Gallon _____
Miles per Gallon _____
Gas Station or Brand _____

_____

Date _____ Mileage_____
Fuel Amount Added _____
Price per Gallon _____
Miles per Gallon _____
Gas Station or Brand _____

_____

Date _____ Mileage_____
Fuel Amount Added _____
Price per Gallon _____
Miles per Gallon _____
Gas Station or Brand _____

_____

Date _____ Mileage_____
Fuel Amount Added _____
Price per Gallon _____
Miles per Gallon _____
Gas Station or Brand _____

_____

Date _____ Mileage_____
Fuel Amount Added _____
Price per Gallon _____
Miles per Gallon _____
Gas Station or Brand _____

_____

Oil Changes

Date _____ Mileage_____
Oil Brand _____
Viscosity _____
Amount Added _____
Condition of Used Oil _____
Oil Filter Brand _____

Date _____ Mileage_____
Oil Brand _____
Viscosity _____
Amount Added _____
Condition of Used Oil _____
Oil Filter Brand _____

Date _____ Mileage_____
Oil Brand _____
Viscosity _____
Amount Added _____
Condition of Used Oil _____
Oil Filter Brand _____

Date _____ Mileage_____
Oil Brand _____
Viscosity _____
Amount Added _____
Condition of Used Oil _____
Oil Filter Brand _____

Date _____ Mileage_____
Oil Brand _____
Viscosity _____
Amount Added _____
Condition of Used Oil _____
Oil Filter Brand _____

Date _____ Mileage_____
Oil Brand _____
Viscosity _____
Amount Added _____
Condition of Used Oil _____
Oil Filter Brand _____

Date _____ Mileage_____
Oil Brand _____
Viscosity _____
Amount Added _____
Condition of Used Oil _____
Oil Filter Brand _____

Date _____ Mileage_____
Oil Brand _____
Viscosity _____
Amount Added _____
Condition of Used Oil _____
Oil Filter Brand _____

Date _____ Mileage_____

Oil Brand _____

Viscosity _____

Amount Added _____

Condition of Used Oil _____

Oil Filter Brand _____

Date _____ Mileage_____

Oil Brand _____

Viscosity _____

Amount Added _____

Condition of Used Oil _____

Oil Filter Brand _____

Date _____ Mileage_____

Oil Brand _____

Viscosity _____

Amount Added _____

Condition of Used Oil _____

Oil Filter Brand _____

Date _____ Mileage_____

Oil Brand _____

Viscosity _____

Amount Added _____

Condition of Used Oil _____

Oil Filter Brand _____

Date _____ Mileage_____

Oil Brand _____

Viscosity _____

Amount Added _____

Condition of Used Oil _____

Oil Filter Brand _____

Date _____ Mileage_____

Oil Brand _____

Viscosity _____

Amount Added _____

Condition of Used Oil _____

Oil Filter Brand _____

Date _____ Mileage_____
Oil Brand _____
Viscosity _____
Amount Added _____
Condition of Used Oil _____
Oil Filter Brand _____

Date _____ Mileage_____
Oil Brand _____
Viscosity _____
Amount Added _____
Condition of Used Oil _____
Oil Filter Brand _____

Date _____ Mileage_____
Oil Brand _____
Viscosity _____
Amount Added _____
Condition of Used Oil _____
Oil Filter Brand _____

Date _____ Mileage_____

Oil Brand _____

Viscosity _____

Amount Added _____

Condition of Used Oil _____

Oil Filter Brand _____

Date _____ Mileage_____

Oil Brand _____

Viscosity _____

Amount Added _____

Condition of Used Oil _____

Oil Filter Brand _____

Date _____ Mileage_____

Oil Brand _____

Viscosity _____

Amount Added _____

Condition of Used Oil _____

Oil Filter Brand _____

Date _____ Mileage_____
Oil Brand _____
Viscosity _____
Amount Added _____
Condition of Used Oil _____
Oil Filter Brand _____

Date _____ Mileage_____
Oil Brand _____
Viscosity _____
Amount Added _____
Condition of Used Oil _____
Oil Filter Brand _____

Date _____ Mileage_____
Oil Brand _____
Viscosity _____
Amount Added _____
Condition of Used Oil _____
Oil Filter Brand _____

Date _____ Mileage_____
Oil Brand _____
Viscosity _____
Amount Added _____
Condition of Used Oil _____
Oil Filter Brand _____

Date _____ Mileage_____
Oil Brand _____
Viscosity _____
Amount Added _____
Condition of Used Oil _____
Oil Filter Brand _____

Date _____ Mileage_____
Oil Brand _____
Viscosity _____
Amount Added _____
Condition of Used Oil _____
Oil Filter Brand _____

Oil Changes

Date _____ Mileage_____
Oil Brand _____
Viscosity _____
Amount Added _____
Condition of Used Oil _____
Oil Filter Brand _____

Date _____ Mileage_____
Oil Brand _____
Viscosity _____
Amount Added _____
Condition of Used Oil _____
Oil Filter Brand _____

Date _____ Mileage_____
Oil Brand _____
Viscosity _____
Amount Added _____
Condition of Used Oil _____
Oil Filter Brand _____

Date _____ Mileage_____
Oil Brand _____
Viscosity _____
Amount Added _____
Condition of Used Oil _____
Oil Filter Brand _____

Date _____ Mileage_____
Oil Brand _____
Viscosity _____
Amount Added _____
Condition of Used Oil _____
Oil Filter Brand _____

Date _____ Mileage_____
Oil Brand _____
Viscosity _____
Amount Added _____
Condition of Used Oil _____
Oil Filter Brand _____

Date _____ Mileage_____

Oil Brand _____

Viscosity _____

Amount Added _____

Condition of Used Oil _____

Oil Filter Brand _____

Date _____ Mileage_____

Oil Brand _____

Viscosity _____

Amount Added _____

Condition of Used Oil _____

Oil Filter Brand _____

Date _____ Mileage_____

Oil Brand _____

Viscosity _____

Amount Added _____

Condition of Used Oil _____

Oil Filter Brand _____

Date _____ Mileage_____
Oil Brand _____
Viscosity _____
Amount Added _____
Condition of Used Oil _____
Oil Filter Brand _____

Date _____ Mileage_____
Oil Brand _____
Viscosity _____
Amount Added _____
Condition of Used Oil _____
Oil Filter Brand _____

Date _____ Mileage_____
Oil Brand _____
Viscosity _____
Amount Added _____
Condition of Used Oil _____
Oil Filter Brand _____

Oil Changes

Date _____ Mileage_____
Oil Brand _____
Viscosity _____
Amount Added _____
Condition of Used Oil _____
Oil Filter Brand _____

Date _____ Mileage_____
Oil Brand _____
Viscosity _____
Amount Added _____
Condition of Used Oil _____
Oil Filter Brand _____

Date _____ Mileage_____
Oil Brand _____
Viscosity _____
Amount Added _____
Condition of Used Oil _____
Oil Filter Brand _____

Date _____ Mileage_____
Oil Brand _____
Viscosity _____
Amount Added _____
Condition of Used Oil _____
Oil Filter Brand _____

Date _____ Mileage_____
Oil Brand _____
Viscosity _____
Amount Added _____
Condition of Used Oil _____
Oil Filter Brand _____

Date _____ Mileage_____
Oil Brand _____
Viscosity _____
Amount Added _____
Condition of Used Oil _____
Oil Filter Brand _____

Date _____ Mileage_____

Oil Brand _____

Viscosity _____

Amount Added _____

Condition of Used Oil _____

Oil Filter Brand _____

Date _____ Mileage_____

Oil Brand _____

Viscosity _____

Amount Added _____

Condition of Used Oil _____

Oil Filter Brand _____

Date _____ Mileage_____

Oil Brand _____

Viscosity _____

Amount Added _____

Condition of Used Oil _____

Oil Filter Brand _____

Transmission Fluid

Date _____ Mileage_____

Amount Added _____

☐ Replaced

Condition of old fluid _____

Brand _____

☐ Filter Replaced

Date _____ Mileage_____

Amount Added _____

☐ Replaced

Condition of old fluid _____

Brand _____

☐ Filter Replaced

Date _____ Mileage_____
Amount Added _____
☐ Replaced
Condition of old fluid _____
Brand _____
☐   Filter Replaced

Date _____ Mileage_____
Amount Added _____
☐ Replaced
Condition of old fluid _____
Brand _____
☐   Filter Replaced

Date _____ Mileage_____
Amount Added _____
☐ Replaced
Condition of old fluid _____
Brand _____
☐   Filter Replaced

Date _____ Mileage_____
Amount Added _____
☐ Replaced
Condition of old fluid _____
Brand _____
☐ Filter Replaced

Date _____ Mileage_____
Amount Added _____
☐ Replaced
Condition of old fluid _____
Brand _____
☐ Filter Replaced

Date _____ Mileage_____
Amount Added _____
☐ Replaced
Condition of old fluid _____
Brand _____
☐ Filter Replaced

Transmission Fluid

Date _____ Mileage_____
Amount Added _____
□ Replaced
Condition of old fluid _____
Brand _____
□ Filter Replaced

Date _____ Mileage_____
Amount Added _____
□ Replaced
Condition of old fluid _____
Brand _____
□ Filter Replaced

Date _____ Mileage_____
Amount Added _____
□ Replaced
Condition of old fluid _____
Brand _____
□ Filter Replaced

Transmission Fluid

Date _____ Mileage_____
Amount Added _____
☐ Replaced
Condition of old fluid _____
Brand _____
☐ Filter Replaced

Date _____ Mileage_____
Amount Added _____
☐ Replaced
Condition of old fluid _____
Brand _____
☐ Filter Replaced

Date _____ Mileage_____
Amount Added _____
☐ Replaced
Condition of old fluid _____
Brand _____
☐ Filter Replaced

Transmission Fluid

Date _____ Mileage_____
Amount Added _____
☐ Replaced
Condition of old fluid _____
Brand _____
☐ Filter Replaced

Date _____ Mileage_____
Amount Added _____
☐ Replaced
Condition of old fluid _____
Brand _____
☐ Filter Replaced

Date _____ Mileage_____
Amount Added _____
☐ Replaced
Condition of old fluid _____
Brand _____
☐ Filter Replaced

Transmission Fluid

Differential Fluid

Date _____ Mileage_____
Amount Added _____
☐ Replaced
Condition of old fluid _____
Brand _____

Date _____ Mileage_____
Amount Added _____
☐ Replaced
Condition of old fluid _____
Brand _____

Date _____ Mileage_____
Amount Added _____
☐ Replaced
Condition of old fluid _____
Brand _____

Date _____ Mileage_____
Amount Added _____
☐ Replaced
Condition of old fluid _____
Brand _____

Date _____ Mileage_____
Amount Added _____
☐ Replaced
Condition of old fluid _____
Brand _____

Date _____ Mileage_____
Amount Added _____
☐ Replaced
Condition of old fluid _____
Brand _____

Date _____ Mileage_____
Amount Added _____
☐ Replaced
Condition of old fluid _____
Brand _____

Date _____ Mileage_____
Amount Added _____
☐ Replaced
Condition of old fluid _____
Brand _____

Differential Fluid

Date _____ Mileage_____

Amount Added _____

☐ Replaced

Condition of old fluid _____

Brand _____

Date _____ Mileage_____

Amount Added _____

☐ Replaced

Condition of old fluid _____

Brand _____

Date _____ Mileage_____

Amount Added _____

☐ Replaced

Condition of old fluid _____

Brand _____

Differential Fluid

Date _____ Mileage_____
Amount Added _____
☐ Replaced
Condition of old fluid _____
Brand _____

Date _____ Mileage_____
Amount Added _____
☐ Replaced
Condition of old fluid _____
Brand _____

Date _____ Mileage_____
Amount Added _____
☐ Replaced
Condition of old fluid _____
Brand _____

Differential Fluid

Date _____ Mileage_____
Amount Added _____
☐ Replaced
Condition of old fluid _____
Brand _____

Date _____ Mileage_____
Amount Added _____
☐ Replaced
Condition of old fluid _____
Brand _____

Date _____ Mileage_____
Amount Added _____
☐ Replaced
Condition of old fluid _____
Brand _____

Tire Maintenance

Record Date, then check box for either or both items
that were performed. Record who performed rotation
and psi as needed.

Date	Mileage	Rotation/Who	psi
____	_____	☐ _____	☐ _____
____	_____	☐ _____	☐ _____
____	_____	☐ _____	☐ _____
____	_____	☐ _____	☐ _____
____	_____	☐ _____	☐ _____
____	_____	☐ _____	☐ _____
____	_____	☐ _____	☐ _____
____	_____	☐ _____	☐ _____
____	_____	☐ _____	☐ _____
____	_____	☐ _____	☐ _____
____	_____	☐ _____	☐ _____
____	_____	☐ _____	☐ _____
____	_____	☐ _____	☐ _____

Tire Maintenance

Date	Mileage	Rotation/Who	psi
_____	_____	☐ _____	☐ _____
_____	_____	☐ _____	☐ _____
_____	_____	☐ _____	☐ _____
_____	_____	☐ _____	☐ _____
_____	_____	☐ _____	☐ _____
_____	_____	☐ _____	☐ _____
_____	_____	☐ _____	☐ _____
_____	_____	☐ _____	☐ _____
_____	_____	☐ _____	☐ _____
_____	_____	☐ _____	☐ _____
_____	_____	☐ _____	☐ _____
_____	_____	☐ _____	☐ _____
_____	_____	☐ _____	☐ _____
_____	_____	☐ _____	☐ _____
_____	_____	☐ _____	☐ _____
		☐	☐

Tire Maintenance

Date	Mileage	Rotation/Who	psi
_____	_____	☐ _____	☐ _____
_____	_____	☐ _____	☐ _____
_____	_____	☐ _____	☐ _____
_____	_____	☐ _____	☐ _____
_____	_____	☐ _____	☐ _____
_____	_____	☐ _____	☐ _____
_____	_____	☐ _____	☐ _____
_____	_____	☐ _____	☐ _____
_____	_____	☐ _____	☐ _____
_____	_____	☐ _____	☐ _____
_____	_____	☐ _____	☐ _____
_____	_____	☐ _____	☐ _____
_____	_____	☐ _____	☐ _____
_____	_____	☐ _____	☐ _____
_____	_____	☐ _____	☐ _____
		☐	☐

Tire Maintenance

Date	Mileage	Rotation/Who	psi
_____	_____	☐ _____	☐ ____
_____	_____	☐ _____	☐ ____
_____	_____	☐ _____	☐ ____
_____	_____	☐ _____	☐ ____
_____	_____	☐ _____	☐ ____
_____	_____	☐ _____	☐ ____
_____	_____	☐ _____	☐ ____
_____	_____	☐ _____	☐ ____
_____	_____	☐ _____	☐ ____
_____	_____	☐ _____	☐ ____
_____	_____	☐ _____	☐ ____
_____	_____	☐ _____	☐ ____
_____	_____	☐ _____	☐ ____
_____	_____	☐ _____	☐ ____
_____	_____	☐ _____	☐ ____
		☐	☐ ____

Tire Maintenance

Tire Maintenance

Date	Mileage	Rotation/Who	psi
_____	_____	☐ _____	☐ _____
_____	_____	☐ _____	☐ _____
_____	_____	☐ _____	☐ _____
_____	_____	☐ _____	☐ _____
_____	_____	☐ _____	☐ _____
_____	_____	☐ _____	☐ _____
_____	_____	☐ _____	☐ _____
_____	_____	☐ _____	☐ _____
_____	_____	☐ _____	☐ _____
_____	_____	☐ _____	☐ _____
_____	_____	☐ _____	☐ _____
_____	_____	☐ _____	☐ _____
_____	_____	☐ _____	☐ _____
_____	_____	☐ _____	☐ _____
_____	_____	☐ _____	☐ _____
		☐	☐

Date	Mileage	Rotation/Who	psi
_____	_____	☐ _____	☐ _____
_____	_____	☐ _____	☐ _____
_____	_____	☐ _____	☐ _____
_____	_____	☐ _____	☐ _____
_____	_____	☐ _____	☐ _____
_____	_____	☐ _____	☐ _____
_____	_____	☐ _____	☐ _____
_____	_____	☐ _____	☐ _____
_____	_____	☐ _____	☐ _____
_____	_____	☐ _____	☐ _____
_____	_____	☐ _____	☐ _____
_____	_____	☐ _____	☐ _____
_____	_____	☐ _____	☐ _____
_____	_____	☐ _____	☐ _____
_____	_____	☐ _____	☐ _____
		☐	☐

Tire Maintenance

Date	Mileage	Rotation/Who		psi	
_____	_____	☐	_____	☐	____
_____	_____	☐	_____	☐	____
_____	_____	☐	_____	☐	____
_____	_____	☐	_____	☐	____
_____	_____	☐	_____	☐	____
_____	_____	☐	_____	☐	____
_____	_____	☐	_____	☐	____
_____	_____	☐	_____	☐	____
_____	_____	☐	_____	☐	____
_____	_____	☐	_____	☐	____
_____	_____	☐	_____	☐	____
_____	_____	☐	_____	☐	____
_____	_____	☐	_____	☐	____
_____	_____	☐	_____	☐	____
_____	_____	☐	_____	☐	____
		☐		☐	

Tire Maintenance

Date	Mileage	Rotation/Who	psi
_____	_____	☐ _____	☐ ____
_____	_____	☐ _____	☐ ____
_____	_____	☐ _____	☐ ____
_____	_____	☐ _____	☐ ____
_____	_____	☐ _____	☐ ____
_____	_____	☐ _____	☐ ____
_____	_____	☐ _____	☐ ____
_____	_____	☐ _____	☐ ____
_____	_____	☐ _____	☐ ____
_____	_____	☐ _____	☐ ____
_____	_____	☐ _____	☐ ____
_____	_____	☐ _____	☐ ____
_____	_____	☐ _____	☐ ____
_____	_____	☐ _____	☐ ____
_____	_____	☐ _____	☐ ____
		☐	☐

Tire Maintenance

Tires

Record Details when you get new tires.
Use the Notes to indicate flat or
puncture.

Date _____ Mileage_____
Replaced/Repaired:
☐ All ☐ Spare ☐ Other
Notes _____
Size _____
Brand _____

Date _____ Mileage_____
Replaced/Repaired:
☐ All ☐ Spare ☐ Other
Notes _____
Size _____
Brand _____

Date _____ Mileage_____
Replaced/Repaired:
 □ All □ Spare □ Other
Notes _____
Size _____
Brand _____

Date _____ Mileage_____
Replaced/Repaired:
 □ All □ Spare □ Other
Notes _____
Size _____
Brand _____

Date _____ Mileage_____
Replaced/Repaired:
 □ All □ Spare □ Other
Notes _____
Size _____
Brand _____

Tires

Date _____ Mileage_____
Replaced/Repaired:
□ All □ Spare □ Other
Notes _____
Size _____
Brand _____

Date _____ Mileage_____
Replaced/Repaired:
□ All □ Spare □ Other
Notes _____
Size _____
Brand _____

Date _____ Mileage_____
Replaced/Repaired:
□ All □ Spare □ Other
Notes _____
Size _____
Brand _____

Tires

Date _____ Mileage_____
Replaced/Repaired:
  □ All   □ Spare   □ Other
Notes _____
Size _____
Brand _____

Date _____ Mileage_____
Replaced/Repaired:
  □ All   □ Spare   □ Other
Notes _____
Size _____
Brand _____

Date _____ Mileage_____
Replaced/Repaired:
  □ All   □ Spare   □ Other
Notes _____
Size _____
Brand _____

Tires

Date _____ Mileage_____
Replaced/Repaired:
  □ All □ Spare □ Other
Notes _____
Size _____
Brand _____

Date _____ Mileage_____
Replaced/Repaired:
  □ All □ Spare □ Other
Notes _____
Size _____
Brand _____

Date _____ Mileage_____
Replaced/Repaired:
  □ All □ Spare □ Other
Notes _____
Size _____
Brand _____

Tires

Date _____ Mileage_____
Replaced/Repaired:
□ All   □ Spare   □ Other
Notes _____
Size _____
Brand _____

Date _____ Mileage_____
Replaced/Repaired:
□ All   □ Spare   □ Other
Notes _____
Size _____
Brand _____

Date _____ Mileage_____
Replaced/Repaired:
□ All   □ Spare   □ Other
Notes _____
Size _____
Brand _____

Tires

Other Maintenance

Date _____ Mileage_____
Maintenance or change performed:

_____

_____

_____

_____

Date _____ Mileage_____
Maintenance or change performed:

_____

_____

_____

_____

Date _____ Mileage_____
Maintenance or change performed:

_____

_____

_____

_____

Date _____ Mileage_____
Maintenance or change performed:

_____

_____

_____

_____

Date _____ Mileage_____
Maintenance or change performed:

_____

_____

_____

_____

Date _____ Mileage_____
Maintenance or change performed:

_____
_____
_____
_____

Date _____ Mileage_____
Maintenance or change performed:

_____
_____
_____
_____

Date _____ Mileage_____
Maintenance or change performed:

_____
_____
_____
_____

Date _____ Mileage _____
Maintenance or change performed:

_____

_____

_____

_____

Date _____ Mileage _____
Maintenance or change performed:

_____

_____

_____

_____

Date _____ Mileage _____
Maintenance or change performed:

_____

_____

_____

_____

Date _____ Mileage_____
Maintenance or change performed:

_____

_____

_____

_____

Date _____ Mileage_____
Maintenance or change performed:

_____

_____

_____

_____

Date _____ Mileage_____
Maintenance or change performed:

_____

_____

_____

_____

Date _____ Mileage_____
Maintenance or change performed:

_____

_____

_____

_____

Date _____ Mileage_____
Maintenance or change performed:

_____

_____

_____

_____

Date _____ Mileage_____
Maintenance or change performed:

_____

_____

_____

_____

Date _____ Mileage_____
Maintenance or change performed:

_____

_____

_____

_____

Date _____ Mileage_____
Maintenance or change performed:

_____

_____

_____

_____

Date _____ Mileage_____
Maintenance or change performed:

_____

_____

_____

_____

Other Maintenance

Date _____ Mileage_____
Maintenance or change performed:

_____

_____

_____

_____

Date _____ Mileage_____
Maintenance or change performed:

_____

_____

_____

_____

Date _____ Mileage_____
Maintenance or change performed:

_____

_____

_____

_____

Date _____ Mileage_____
Maintenance or change performed:

_____

_____

_____

_____

Date _____ Mileage_____
Maintenance or change performed:

_____

_____

_____

_____

Date _____ Mileage_____
Maintenance or change performed:

_____

_____

_____

_____

Date _____ Mileage_____
Maintenance or change performed:

_____

_____

_____

_____

Date _____ Mileage_____
Maintenance or change performed:

_____

_____

_____

_____

Date _____ Mileage_____
Maintenance or change performed:

_____

_____

_____

_____

Other Maintenance

Date _____ Mileage_____
Maintenance or change performed:

_____

_____

_____

Date _____ Mileage_____

Maintenance or change performed:

_____

_____

_____

Date _____ Mileage_____
Maintenance or change performed:

_____

_____

_____

Date _____ Mileage_____
Maintenance or change performed:

_____

_____

_____

_____

Date _____ Mileage_____
Maintenance or change performed:

_____

_____

_____

_____

Date _____ Mileage_____
Maintenance or change performed:

_____

_____

_____

_____

Date _____ Mileage_____
Maintenance or change performed:

_____

_____

_____

_____

Date _____ Mileage_____
Maintenance or change performed:

_____

_____

_____

_____

Date _____ Mileage_____
Maintenance or change performed:

_____

_____

_____

_____

Other Maintenance

Date _____ Mileage_____
Maintenance or change performed:

_____

_____

_____

_____

Date _____ Mileage_____
Maintenance or change performed:

_____

_____

_____

_____

Date _____ Mileage_____
Maintenance or change performed:

_____

_____

_____

_____

Date _____ Mileage_____
Maintenance or change performed:

_____

_____

_____

_____

Date _____ Mileage_____
Maintenance or change performed:

_____

_____

_____

_____

Other Maintenance

Date _____ Mileage_____
Maintenance or change performed:

_____

_____

_____

_____

Date _____ Mileage_____
Maintenance or change performed:

_____

_____

_____

_____

Date _____ Mileage_____
Maintenance or change performed:

_____

_____

_____

_____

Date _____ Mileage_____
Maintenance or change performed:

_____

_____

_____

_____

Date _____ Mileage_____
Maintenance or change performed:

_____

_____

_____

_____

Date _____ Mileage_____
Maintenance or change performed:

_____

_____

_____

_____

Date _____ Mileage_____
Maintenance or change performed:

_____

_____

_____

_____

Other Maintenance

Date _____ Mileage_____
Maintenance or change performed:

_____

_____

_____

_____

Date _____ Mileage_____
Maintenance or change performed:

_____

_____

_____

_____

Date _____ Mileage_____
Maintenance or change performed:

_____

_____

_____

_____

Date _____ Mileage_____
Maintenance or change performed:

_____
_____
_____
_____

Date _____ Mileage_____
Maintenance or change performed:

_____
_____
_____
_____

Date _____ Mileage_____
Maintenance or change performed:

_____
_____
_____
_____

Other Maintenance

Date _____ Mileage_____
Maintenance or change performed:

_____

_____

_____

_____

Date _____ Mileage_____
Maintenance or change performed:

_____

_____

_____

_____

Date _____ Mileage_____
Maintenance or change performed:

_____

_____

_____

_____

Date _____ Mileage_____
Maintenance or change performed:

_____
_____
_____
_____

Date _____ Mileage_____
Maintenance or change performed:

_____
_____
_____
_____

Date _____ Mileage_____
Maintenance or change performed:

_____
_____
_____
_____

Other Maintenance

Date _____ Mileage_____
Maintenance or change performed:

_____

_____

_____

_____

Date _____ Mileage_____
Maintenance or change performed:

_____

_____

_____

_____

Date _____ Mileage_____
Maintenance or change performed:

_____

_____

_____

_____

Date _____ Mileage_____
Maintenance or change performed:

_____

_____

_____

_____

Date _____ Mileage_____
Maintenance or change performed:

_____

_____

_____

_____

Date _____ Mileage_____
Maintenance or change performed:

_____

_____

_____

_____

Other Maintenance

Date _____ Mileage_____
Maintenance or change performed:

_____

_____

_____

_____

Date _____ Mileage_____
Maintenance or change performed:

_____

_____

_____

_____

Date _____ Mileage_____
Maintenance or change performed:

_____

_____

_____

_____

Date _____ Mileage_____
Maintenance or change performed:

_____

_____

_____

_____

Date _____ Mileage_____
Maintenance or change performed:

_____

_____

_____

_____

Date _____ Mileage_____
Maintenance or change performed:

_____

_____

_____

_____

Other Maintenance

Date _____ Mileage_____
Maintenance or change performed:

_____

_____

_____

_____

Date _____ Mileage_____
Maintenance or change performed:

_____

_____

_____

_____

Date _____ Mileage_____
Maintenance or change performed:

_____

_____

_____

_____

Date _____ Mileage_____
Maintenance or change performed:

_____

_____

_____

_____

Date _____ Mileage_____
Maintenance or change performed:

_____

_____

_____

_____

Date _____ Mileage_____
Maintenance or change performed:

_____

_____

_____

_____

Other Maintenance

Date _____ Mileage_____
Maintenance or change performed:

_____

_____

_____

_____

Date _____ Mileage_____
Maintenance or change performed:

_____

_____

_____

_____

Date _____ Mileage_____
Maintenance or change performed:

_____

_____

_____

_____

Other Maintenance

Date _____ Mileage_____
Maintenance or change performed:

_____
_____
_____
_____

Date _____ Mileage_____
Maintenance or change performed:

_____
_____
_____
_____

Other Maintenance

Date _____ Mileage_____
Maintenance or change performed:

_____
_____
_____
_____

Date _____ Mileage_____
Maintenance or change performed:

_____

_____

_____

_____

Date _____ Mileage_____
Maintenance or change performed:

_____

_____

_____

_____

Date _____ Mileage_____
Maintenance or change performed:

_____

_____

_____

_____

Date _____ Mileage_____
Maintenance or change performed:

_____
_____
_____
_____

Date _____ Mileage_____
Maintenance or change performed:

_____
_____
_____
_____

Date _____ Mileage_____
Maintenance or change performed:

_____
_____
_____
_____

Other Maintenance

Date _____ Mileage_____
Maintenance or change performed:

_____

_____

_____

_____

Date _____ Mileage_____
Maintenance or change performed:

_____

_____

_____

_____

Date _____ Mileage_____
Maintenance or change performed:

_____

_____

_____

_____

Date _____ Mileage_____
Maintenance or change performed:

_____

_____

_____

_____

Date _____ Mileage_____
Maintenance or change performed:

_____

_____

_____

_____

Date _____ Mileage_____
Maintenance or change performed:

_____

_____

_____

_____

Date _____ Mileage_____
Maintenance or change performed:

_____
_____
_____
_____

Date _____ Mileage_____
Maintenance or change performed:

_____
_____
_____
_____

Date _____ Mileage_____
Maintenance or change performed:

_____
_____
_____
_____

Other Maintenance

Date _____ Mileage_____
Maintenance or change performed:

_____

_____

_____

_____

Date _____ Mileage_____
Maintenance or change performed:

_____

_____

_____

_____

Date _____ Mileage_____
Maintenance or change performed:

_____

_____

_____

_____

Date _____ Mileage_____
Maintenance or change performed:

_____

_____

_____

_____

Date _____ Mileage_____
Maintenance or change performed:

_____

_____

_____

_____

Date _____ Mileage_____
Maintenance or change performed:

_____

_____

_____

_____

Date _____ Mileage_____
Maintenance or change performed:

_____

_____

_____

_____

Date _____ Mileage_____
Maintenance or change performed:

_____

_____

_____

_____

Other Maintenance

Date _____ Mileage_____
Maintenance or change performed:

_____

_____

_____

_____

Date _____ Mileage_____
Maintenance or change performed:

_____

_____

_____

_____

Date _____ Mileage_____
Maintenance or change performed:

_____

_____

_____

_____

Date _____ Mileage_____
Maintenance or change performed:

_____

_____

_____

_____

Date _____ Mileage_____
Maintenance or change performed:

_____

_____

_____

_____

Date _____ Mileage_____
Maintenance or change performed:

_____

_____

_____

_____

Date _____ Mileage_____
Maintenance or change performed:

_____

_____

_____

_____

Other Maintenance

Date _____ Mileage_____
Maintenance or change performed:

_____

_____

_____

_____

Date _____ Mileage_____
Maintenance or change performed:

_____

_____

_____

_____

Date _____ Mileage_____
Maintenance or change performed:

_____

_____

_____

_____

Date _____ Mileage_____
Maintenance or change performed:

_____

_____

_____

_____

Date _____ Mileage_____
Maintenance or change performed:

_____

_____

_____

_____

Date _____ Mileage_____
Maintenance or change performed:

_____

_____

_____

_____

Other Maintenance

Date _____ Mileage_____
Maintenance or change performed:

_____

_____

_____

_____

Date _____ Mileage_____
Maintenance or change performed:

_____

_____

_____

_____

Other Maintenance

Date _____ Mileage_____
Maintenance or change performed:

_____

_____

_____

_____

Date _____ Mileage_____
Maintenance or change performed:

_____
_____
_____
_____

Date _____ Mileage_____
Maintenance or change performed:

_____
_____
_____
_____

Date _____ Mileage_____
Maintenance or change performed:

_____
_____
_____
_____

Other Maintenance

Date _____ Mileage_____
Maintenance or change performed:

_____

_____

_____

_____

Date _____ Mileage_____
Maintenance or change performed:

_____

_____

_____

_____

Date _____ Mileage_____
Maintenance or change performed:

_____

_____

_____

_____

Other Maintenance

Graphs

These grids are here in case you want to graph miles per gallon, price per gallon or something else. (Or you can make your own graph and stick it here.)

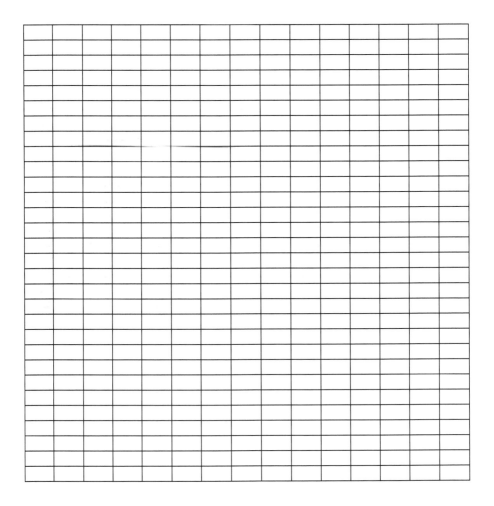

Contacts

People you meet who did or might do work on your vehicle in the future, or anyone you meet related to your vehicle.

Name _____

Phone Number _____

Email/website _____

Work or Specialty _____

Other Notes _____

_____

Name _____

Phone Number _____

Email/website _____

Work or Specialty _____

Other Notes _____

_____

Name _____

Phone Number _____

Email/website _____

Work or Specialty _____

Other Notes _____

_____

Name _____

Phone Number _____

Email/website _____

Work or Specialty _____

Other Notes _____

_____

Name _____

Phone Number _____

Email/website _____

Work or Specialty _____

Other Notes _____

_____

Name _____

Phone Number _____

Email/website _____

Work or Specialty _____

Other Notes _____

_____

Name _____

Phone Number _____

Email/website _____

Work or Specialty _____

Other Notes _____

_____

Name _____

Phone Number _____

Email/website _____

Work or Specialty _____

Other Notes _____

_____

Contacts

Name _____

Phone Number _____

Email/website _____

Work or Specialty _____

Other Notes _____

_____

Name _____

Phone Number _____

Email/website _____

Work or Specialty _____

Other Notes _____

_____

Name _____

Phone Number _____

Email/website _____

Work or Specialty _____

Other Notes _____

_____

Name _____

Phone Number _____

Email/website _____

Work or Specialty _____

Other Notes _____

_____

Name _____

Phone Number _____

Email/website _____

Work or Specialty _____

Other Notes _____

_____

Name _____

Phone Number _____

Email/website _____

Work or Specialty _____

Other Notes _____

_____

Contacts

Name _____

Phone Number _____

Email/website _____

Work or Specialty _____

Other Notes _____

_____

Name _____

Phone Number _____

Email/website _____

Work or Specialty _____

Other Notes _____

_____

Name _____

Phone Number _____

Email/website _____

Work or Specialty _____

Other Notes _____

_____

Contacts

Made in the USA
San Bernardino, CA
05 May 2017